YINKA ILORI CHAIRMAN

JAREH DAS
FOREWORD

Take a seat. In these collections, as in life, no chair is ever just a chair. It holds who we are and who we are becoming. Chairs have always existed as silent witnesses to our everyday rituals, arguments, dreams, and celebrations. They prop us up, gather us together, or remind us of absence when empty. For Yinka Ilori, chairs are not just functional objects but also vessels of memory, symbols of cultural inheritance, and canvases for wider storytelling. His design practice is rooted in his Nigerian-British heritage, insisting that design can carry joy, honour ancestry, and reimagine how we sit together in the present.

Growing up in a Nigerian household in London, Ilori recalls the everyday chairs that defined the rhythm of domestic life and community life: the ubiquitous plastic chair pulled out for family gatherings, the high-backed seat reserved for elders, or the padded church pew that bore the weight of prayer and song every Sunday. These objects seemed ordinary at the time, yet they were always charged with meaning. They revealed hierarchy, intimacy, and aspiration in equal measure. A child might perch on the edge of a stool to listen in on adult conversations, while a father or pastor's seat marked authority. In Nigeria, across its diaspora and beyond, chairs are never neutral. They carry power, memory, and imagination.

This is where the layered resonance of the *Chairman* becomes vital. In Nigerian Pidgin, "Chairman" is a term of respect, sometimes sincere, sometimes teasing. It can signal authority, leadership, or simply swagger. The "Chairman" is the *big man*, the *oga*, the *odogwu*. It commands respect, but it can also be your friend acting important, your cousin showing off a new car, or the area elder who convenes a meeting. In everyday parlance, it is both playful and profound, a reminder of how language transforms simple words into markers of belonging. To call someone "Chairman", as Julianknxx reminds us in this book's epilogue,(p 117) is to grant them a symbolic seat of power, even if only just for the moment.

Ilori has built a career for over a decade around amplifying this tension between the everyday and the exalted. His chairs straddle the line between utility and spectacle, improvisation and monument. They draw on Yoruba parables, West African textiles, and the improvisational genius of Lagos street life, while also speaking directly to the multicultural fabric of London. His is a practice of joyful hybridity, rooted in the lessons of both inheritance and adaptation.

The instinct to reuse and reimagine is also central. Nigerian households, like many across the Global South, have long practised the art of making do, mending broken legs, repurposing discarded furniture, or combining parts to extend an object's life. For Ilori, upcycling is not just sustainability rhetoric; it is heritage, a lived experience of transformation. His early works emerged from scavenging discarded chairs from the streets of London and recombining them into new, multicoloured forms. This was not only about saving waste, but also about retelling stories, finding beauty in the broken, and imagining new futures from overlooked pasts.

Here, Martino Gamper's project *100 Chairs in 100 Days* is a key catalyst. By reshaping discarded chairs into inventive hybrids, Gamper exposed the narrative possibilities of everyday furniture. For Ilori, this opened a door to thinking critically about design as a form of storytelling. He took this principle and infused it with Nigerian parables, African textiles, colour sensibilities, and diasporic humour. The result was an aesthetic that was not merely functional but also narrative, with each chair serving as a character, a proverb, or a chapter in a larger story of cultural resilience.

Mentorship and influence are also woven through Ilori's journey. At university, Jane Atfield's *Our Chair* project challenged students to reimagine a standard *RCP2* chair (Img. 1) with recycled plastics, asking them to confront questions of sustainability and identity. Atfield's insistence that material choices are both ethical and aesthetic planted seeds that continue to grow in Ilori's practice. To upcycle is to acknowledge both scarcity and creativity; it is to insist that design has social, political, and ecological stakes. Ilori has carried this conviction into every project, from his first reassembled chairs to public commissions that reshape entire streetscapes with colour.

Img. 1: "RCP2" Chair by Jane Atfield, 1992. Photo: Sean Davidson.

Colour itself is Ilori's most exuberant language. His palette is not merely decorative but communicative, drawing from textiles, the bustle of Lagos markets, and the visual vibrancy of multicultural inner-city London. He uses colour to craft spaces of joy, to resist drab conformity, and to assert presence. In his hands, colour is emotion, rhythm, and resistance. It becomes a way of affirming that design can be a source of collective happiness as much as it is a tool for critical reflection.

Chairs also stage power. The Nigerian photographer George Osodi captured this vividly in his portraits of Nigerian monarchs, *Nigerian Monarchs* (2006–2017), which challenge colonial-era photographs by instead capturing regional rulers in his home country, where thrones become extensions of sovereignty, embodying both theatricality and authority. To sit on such a throne is to be seen, revered, perhaps even feared. Ilori's work engages with this history while reimagining it. He celebrates the dignity of both throne and stool, acknowledging that every seat can carry majesty. By elevating discarded furniture into sculptural statements, he collapses hierarchies: the humble plastic or wooden chair, when reimagined, can be as regal as any gilded throne. (Img. 2)

Img. 2: HM Ogiame Atuwatse III, The Olu of Warri Kingdom, 2022. Photo: George Osodi. Courtesy of the artist and TAFETA.

At the same time, Ilori's chairs remind us of the importance of community. To gather around chairs is to gather around stories. The scratches, stitches, and welds of a chair become archives of touch and time. In this sense, his practice is not just about furniture, but about relationships—between people, between cultures, and between past and present. He designs not just for the solitary sitter but for collective memory. His chairs are invitations: sit, converse, imagine, belong. This is perhaps why Ilori's work resonates so strongly in both gallery and street contexts. In museums, his chairs disrupt conventional design narratives by foregrounding diasporic joy and play. In public spaces, they animate everyday life, transforming crossings, staircases, and playgrounds into theatres of colour and connection. His designs reflect a philosophy that rejects the separation between art and life. For Ilori, the chair is not only an object to be looked at but also a proposition about how we might live together.

The question then becomes: *What stories do our chairs tell? Who gets to sit, and how? What happens when we elevate the overlooked and dignify the ordinary?* Ilori's work urges us to consider these questions. He demonstrates that design is never neutral, that even the most familiar objects carry histories of power, exclusion, aspiration, and joy. By reframing chairs as storytellers, he expands the possibilities of what design can mean and who it can serve.

As you turn these pages, **take a seat**. Consider the thrones, stools, and hybrids assembled here, reimagined by Yinka Ilori's chairs. Remember the childhood chairs that shaped your own sense of self, the gatherings they witnessed, the authority or intimacy they signalled. Reflect on how a chair might carry a proverb, a song, or a joke. And allow Ilori's practice to remind you that design is not only about objects but about the lives we live in their presence.

A chair is never just a chair. It is a memory, a story, a community, a throne. In Ilori's hands, it is also a vision of joy, resilience, and possibility.

Welcome to the world of the **Chairman**.

YINKA ILORI & JANE ATFIELD CONVERSATION

Interview conducted and edited by Jareh Das

Img. 3: Jane Atfield and Yinka Ilori, 2025. Photo: Kane Hulse.

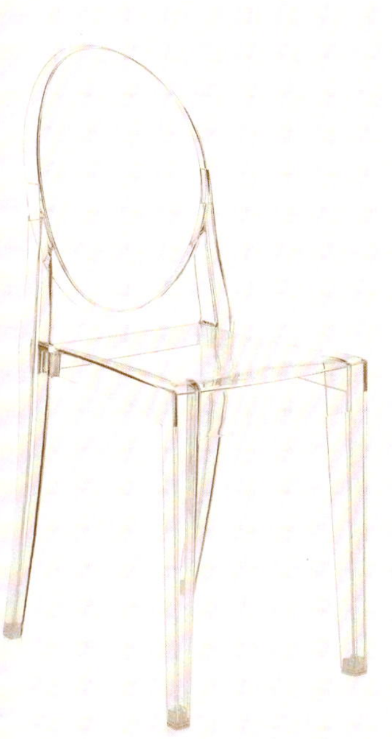

Img. 4: "Victoria Ghost Chair" by Philippe Starck, manufactured by Kartell. Courtesy Kartell.

BA Furniture and Product Design
Level One
3D Design Module 1: PM 1030C
Project 3
2008/09

HYBRID

This project is inspired by the possibilities of combining items of worn out or discarded furniture into a desirable and useful object. This transformation in turn will then act as a starting point to explore how a one-off piece can inspire and be translated for mass production.
Also by looking at existing structures within furniture archetypes, you will be considering and documenting how your new pieces are constructed.

Part 1: Individual

There are four main categories of furniture: chairs, beds, tables and shelving which relate to basic functions of sitting, sleeping, eating/writing and storage. Most furniture can fit into one of these categories and initially you are requested to find a wide range of examples showing the extent of each category eg chairs: sofas to benches and stools. Consider carefully the structure of the pieces you have chosen, what materials they are made of and how their individual components are connected together. Which examples do you like or dislike and why?
Represent this research visually on A3 sheets for studio pin up and discussion.

Part 2: Group

1) You will be working in groups of 3. Your starting point is to find a single discarded item of furniture, each of you from a different category. This might be something you have at home and are longing to get rid of or something from a skip or local junk shop. Brick Lane Market on a Sunday morning is a good place to look.

2) Photograph each piece separately and then draw it as a technical drawing at 1:5. Work with your partners please to find a way of combining your individual pieces into a single item of hybrid furniture. You need to retain the 3 individual functions, but you are free to use the complete objects or deconstruct them down into component parts. Consider how and where this new combination

Img. 5: "Our Chair" Brief (later titled "Hybrid") by Jane Atfield, 2006. Courtesy Jane Atfield.

Q: Can you each recall your first impressions of one another? What stood out, either in Yinka's early approach or Jane's teaching style?

Jane Atfield: I remember Yinka's big smile! He was a lovely student—enthusiastic and shining with positivity, curiosity, and energy. He brought a real spark to the studio, always open to new ideas and eager to experiment.

Yinka Ilori: I had two tutors, Jez Bradley and Jane Atfield. Jez was a real design geek. I remember he was really proud of the "Victoria Ghost Chair" (Img. 4) by Philippe Starck in the studio. Jane, on the other hand, taught me once or twice a week. She always had a calm, warm demeanour about her, but was also somewhat elusive, not talking much. However, whenever you engaged with her, it was always positive and calming. She took her time to explain things and helped you find meaning in design. I didn't see her much, but every interaction was positive.

Q: The "Our Chair" project was inspired by Martino Gamper's "100 Chairs in 100 Days". Within the "Our Chair" brief, (Img. 5) why did you choose this reference, Jane and Yinka? What did it spark in you at the time?

J.A.: I wrote the "Our Chair" project in 2003 for the first-year student module, but Martino did not inspire it! He was motivated by the project's approach and went on to design his own hybrid chairs, which later led to the book "100 Chairs in 100 Days". The project was intended to encourage furniture that reflected wider environmental and social issues, including waste, reuse, and consumerism, and how discarded objects could be transformed into something meaningful and symbolic of the times. Looking back, the project was a reaction to the hyper-styled, sleek furniture celebrated in the 1980s. Also, by deconstructing the old chairs, the students would learn how chairs were put together and their component parts.

Y.I.: When I got the brief for "Our Chair", I thought, "This is about something that belongs to us, a collective, not just one person." It made me think more deeply about chairs as objects for the community, not just individuals. At home, my parents had their own special chairs. My dad had his chair; my mum had hers. It was personal, almost like a procession. The brief also mentioned Martino Gamper's "100 Chairs in 100 Days", which we researched as inspiration. My collaborator was Ronald, a friend from Guyana who was great at making furniture. We planned to set up a studio together after university, but our ideas diverged. We're still good friends, though.

Q: Yinka, how did the act of dismantling and reassembling old chairs challenge your understanding of function and identity in design?

Y.I.: For me, I started experimenting with chairs early on, looking at how they're used in different cultural spaces. In a Nigerian home, people often put their legs up on chairs to relax; in a British home, perhaps not. Chairs also represent hierarchy and status. I'd take off the legs of chairs, making them smaller; suddenly, they look like kids' chairs or seem less functional. It changes how you see their purpose. I always say chairs "talk" and they absorb the stories and environments they're in. One chair from a pub, surrounded by loud, happy people; another from a house in Archway, North London, involved in a different scene. I loved the idea of giving these objects a new identity, layering stories without erasing the old ones. Jane's brief was clear: use every component, every screw, bolt, hinge, in the new object. (Img. 6)

Img. 6: Deconstructed parts of "Two Become One". Courtesy Setworks.

Q: Jane, your RCP2 chair from 1992 is a pioneering work in sustainable design. How do you see its relevance in today's design education and Yinka's practice?

J.A.: Sustainability is, in theory, embedded in today's design and production, although we are still so far away from where we need to be, with consumer culture being the dominant force. Desire rather than need is often the dominant discourse. There are relatively few people thriving in the world, and design is more often than not complicit in this, working within dysfunctional political structures, i.e., late-stage capitalism. The RCP2 chair was designed to utilise recycled plastic transparently and honestly, rather than hiding the material's origins. (Img. 1 / p 6) It always intrigued me that sometimes people thought the multi coloured recycled plastic back in the '90s, was a pattern painted onto wood, rather than being inherent to the material and process.

I see echoes of this in Yinka's work, in his use of colour, material, and narrative to challenge assumptions and provoke thought. The conversation around sustainability is more urgent than ever, and I believe both our practices, in different ways, aim to address this issue.

Q: Yinka, in your "Parables for Happiness" exhibition, you included Jane's RCP2 chair. What does that gesture say about how you view lineage, legacy, and influence in your work?

Y.I.: Jane doesn't get enough credit for what she did, and her work changed design in so many ways, especially as a woman in a male-dominated field. She was one of the first to introduce recycled chairs, now at the V&A, inspiring many designers today. Including her chair in my exhibition (Img. 7) was about celebrating her legacy and highlighting her impact, especially her focus on sustainability. For me, it's about acknowledging the people who came before, who opened doors and made it possible for designers like me to tell our stories.

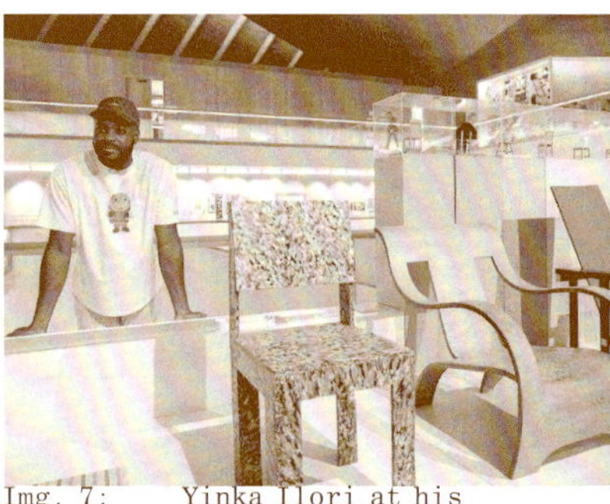

Img. 7: Yinka Ilori at his Design Museum exhibition "Parables for Happiness", 2022, next to the "RCP2" chair by Jane Atfield, amongst chairs. Photo: Stephen Chung / Alamy.

Q: How important is storytelling in furniture design, and how did that begin to take root in your early collaborations or critiques at university?

Y.I.: Storytelling is everything for me. Chairs, for example, aren't just objects; they're witnesses to life, to family, to community. At university, I began to realise how design could be a means of telling stories about my heritage, which is a blend of British and Nigerian roots. Jane encouraged us to find meaning in design, to look for the stories hidden in objects. That's something that's stayed with me ever since.

J. A.: I always looked for students who brought their own stories and perspectives into their work. With Yinka, it was clear from the outset that he was interested in narrative, using design to explore identity and culture. That's what makes his work so powerful.

Q: Jane, what did you see in Yinka's student work that indicated a unique design language emerging? Was there a particular moment that stays with you?

J. A.: Yinka was always enthusiastic and curious, but what stood out was his willingness to experiment and to bring his own background into the work. He wasn't afraid to use colour, to reference his heritage, or to challenge conventions. There was a moment when he brought in a chair from home, and you could see how much it meant to him, not just as a design object, but as a piece of his story. That's when I knew he was developing a unique voice.

Q: Yinka, your use of colour, culture, and community is now a signature. Can you trace elements of that back to your student days, or to conversations you had with Jane?

Y. I.: Definitely. My mum was a proud Nigerian. If you cut her, you'd see green, white, green (Nigeria's national flag colours). Growing up, I didn't feel much pride in being Nigerian, but at university, I sought out designers I could relate to, such as Yinka Shonibare and David Adjaye. Seeing how they wove their heritage into their work inspired me. Jane encouraged us to bring ourselves into our work, to use design as a way to celebrate who we are. That's where my use of colour, culture, and community really started to take shape.

Q: In design education today, what are the most urgent lessons around sustainability, especially given your early emphasis on recycled materials, Jane, and your public commissions, Yinka?

J. A.: Sustainability is still not where it needs to be. Consumer culture is so dominant, and design often ends up serving that rather than challenging it. We need to think more critically about what we make, why we make it, and who benefits. Plastic production should be massively scaled down and used only for essential things like medical equipment. The harmful effects of plastics on health and the environment are now widely recognised.

Design education should focus on these issues, encouraging students to question the status quo and explore genuinely sustainable new ways of working.

Y. I.: For me, sustainability is about more than just materials. It's about community, about making things that last, that have meaning. In my public commissions, I try to create spaces and objects that bring people together, that tell stories, that make people feel seen. That's a kind of sustainability, too.

Q: If you were to co-design a chair together today, what would it look like, and what story would it tell?

J. A.: I've been immersed in studying the plant world these last few years, including how they grow and interact with each other and what they evoke. We could design fabric patterns together, derived from research into Nigerian plants such as the yellow trumpet flower and purple plume grass, and use them to upholster archetypal English chairs like the Windsor. Maybe we'd go to Kew Gardens and the fantastic William Morris Gallery in Walthamstow for inspiration.... Alternatively, we could visit the British Museum together to look at the chairs in the Africa Gallery. How about arranging for a Yoruba throne to be returned to Nigeria? The design element would come from decontextualising its display, outlining the full colonial story and why the throne had ended up in London. Or I'd suggest exploring how British plastic production is rocketing and why British plastic waste is still now being exported to Nigeria. We could also study traditional Nigerian wooden chair carvings and consider contemporary versions that represent things we feel are relevant today, embracing Yinka's love of narrative, colour, and patterns. How could the chair communicate ideas about status, heritage, colonialism, environmentalism, inequality, and community?

Img. 8: Monobloc Chair. Courtesy Victoria and Albert Museum.

Y. I.: I love that! For me, it's about telling a story, about heritage, about community, about reclaiming history. I'd want to use colour, pattern, and recycled materials to create something that feels joyful but also has layers of meaning. Maybe the chair could travel, collecting stories from different places, or be used in a public space where people can add their own marks to it. It would be a living object, constantly changing, always telling new stories.

Q: Chairs are often overlooked as everyday objects, but they carry deep associations with power, domesticity, social class, and cultural rituals (particularly in non-Western, African, Nigerian, and diasporic contexts that Yinka comes from). How do you each think about the symbolic function of the chair, both in the home and in broader society?

Img. 9: Women on a Monobloc Chair at a hair salon in Juba, South Sudan. Photo: Sara Hylton.

Y. I.: In church, plastic chairs (Img. 8 / 9 / 10) bring people together and are a symbol of hope and community. On the altar, you see elegant chairs for apostles, symbolising hierarchy. In public spaces, chairs and benches encourage togetherness. In Nigeria, chairs are everywhere. Under trees, in communities, at parties. They comfort, hold secrets, and offer support. Chairs are spiritual objects.

It's all about power, hierarchy, and status. Why do we think some chairs are more powerful than others? I experimented with scale, such as my 2.7-metre chair at Royal Docks (Img. 11), to challenge these ideas, especially in Nigerian culture, where respect is highly valued. Humour is also important in my work, as it helps people digest deeper messages about identity, race, and culture.

J. A.: Chairs are loaded with symbolism. Who gets to sit where, who is invited to the table, and who is left out. They're about power, about belonging, about comfort and discomfort.

Img. 10: Monobloc chairs at a wedding in Nairobi. Photo: Faith Mbaria.

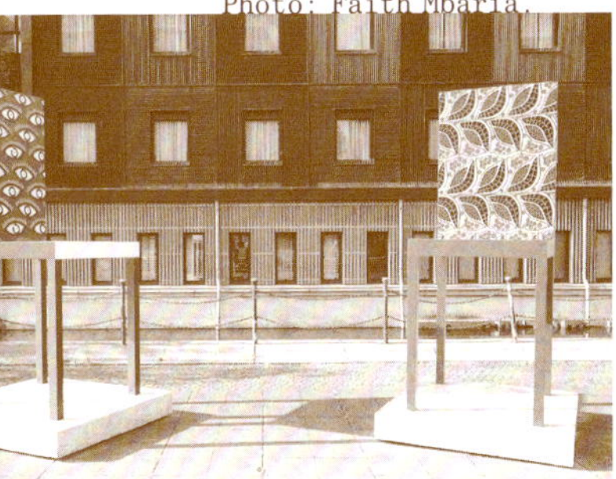

Img. 11: The Line Art Walk, London, 2023. Photo: Steven Chung / Pinep Media.

In my own work, I've tried to use the chair as a way to discuss waste, value, and what we choose to keep versus what we discard. Chairs can be monuments, stages, or declarations of power. They're never just objects.

YINKA ILORI & MARTINO GAMPER CONVERSATION

Yinka Ilori: Martino, your "100 Chairs in 100 Days" project was foundational for me. It really changed how I thought about design. What was your intention behind that project, and what conversations were you hoping to spark at the time?

Martino Gamper: That project has a bit of a winding origin story! It started at the V&A in 2002, where my friend and I were invited to create something creative for a summer fair. We'd been collecting old furniture off the street, and at the fair, we just started making things on the spot, no sketches, no plans, just grabbing materials and seeing what happened. It was so much more immediate and fun than the usual design process.

Later, a friend challenged me to make 100 chairs in 100 days, and it got published before I'd even started, so I had to do it! For me, it was never about making something commercial. It was about research, about seeing what a chair could be, and about letting go of perfectionism. I wanted to explore what happens when you combine different eras and materials, and to see what stories emerge when you work fast and trust your instincts. I think the project was about process, improvisation, and letting creativity flow without overthinking. It was a way to challenge myself and, hopefully, to encourage others to see design as something open and experimental.

Y. I.: We both started out working with discarded or overlooked objects. What drew you to these things no one wanted, and how did you start to reimagine their stories?

M. G.: Honestly, it was a mix of necessity and curiosity. When you're starting, you use what you can find. But I quickly realised there's something special about working with found objects. Each piece has its own history, its own scars and stories. When you put materials from different times together, they start to "talk" to each other.

You also have to let go of your own style a bit, because the materials push back; they have their own ideas. It's about being creative with what you have, not just what you plan. That's where the magic happens.

Y. I.: Chairs seem to return again and again in both our practices. Why do you think the chair holds such enduring symbolic and functional power?

M. G.: Chairs are fascinating because, despite all the changes in technology and society, they haven't really changed that much. I mean, I'm sitting in a chair right now, talking to you, and people have been doing that–sitting, thinking, talking–for centuries.

A chair is so close to our bodies that it literally holds us in place. It's where we focus, where we share stories, where we rest. You can trace the history of the world through chairs; their styles, materials, and uses reflect so much about culture, status, and even politics.

There's something universal and deeply personal about chairs. They're simple, but they carry so much meaning.

Y. I.: You trained under the renowned artist, Michelangelo Pistoletto, and have a strong background in sculpture. How has that sculptural approach influenced your thinking about function in furniture, and maybe even this broader conversation between art and design?

M. G.: I left school at a young age and learned by doing. First as an apprentice, then at art school in Vienna. Pistoletto was amazing because he encouraged us to follow our interests, not just to be "artists". I thought I was doing sculpture, but I was also making furniture. He never pressed us on whether something was functional or not; it was more about what we were trying to express. That freedom to blur the lines between art and design really shaped me. It made me realise you don't have to choose; you can let your work exist in that in-between space.

Y. I.: After I encountered your work, especially "100 Chairs in 100 Days " (Img. 12), I started thinking differently about how objects could tell stories, especially for an early Okra Chair I made in 2012. (Img. 13) How do you think narrative and memory, whether personal or cultural, can be embedded in design?

M. G.: When you combine materials from different times or places, you're creating a conversation between them. There is history, memory, and story in every object, even if you don't see it right away. Sometimes you only realise the meaning much later, when you look back. Design can absolutely be a form of storytelling, even if the story isn't apparent at first. Sometimes it's about memory, sometimes about culture, sometimes just about the journey of making.

Y. I.: We both seem to resist the idea of design being purely functional or perfect. How do you think about imperfection, mismatch, and improvisation as principles?

M. G.: Imperfection is where creativity happens! If you wait for the perfect idea, you'll never make anything. I love the comparison to freestyle rap battles, as sometimes the best ideas come when you're just responding in the moment, not overthinking.

Design needs more poetry and less sterility. Computers and sketches can make things too clean, too rational. The best work often comes from embracing the unexpected.

Y. I.: I've always been drawn to colour as a way to tell stories and challenge taste. You also embrace vibrant, eclectic forms. Is this a joyful resistance to minimalism?

M. G.: Honestly, I have to give credit to my wife, Francis, for the colour in my work.

Y. I.: A chair isn't just a seat; it's a social marker. How do you think about its cultural and political dimensions?

M. G.: Chairs reflect status, hierarchy, and culture. In some places, the type of chair you have says a lot about you, whether it's in the home, at a party, or in church. They're part of rituals, gatherings, and everyday life.

They're loaded with meaning, far beyond their function.

Y. I.: What are your thoughts on how design education can better

Img. 12: "100 Chairs in 100 Days and Its 100 Ways: Martino Gamper", 2007. Courtesy Martino Gamper & Dent-De-Leone.

Img. 13: "Okra" Chair by Yinka Ilori, inspired by origami, 2012. Courtesy Yinka Ilori.

encourage experimentation with reuse, storytelling, and material history?

M. G.: I was lucky to study at a time when design education was really open-minded. We had a lot of studio work, hands-on making, and encouragement to think outside the box. Students need their own space, their own desk, and access to workshops.

It's also important to mix disciplines, such as art, design, and craft, so that students can learn from one another. And get out of the classroom! Some of my most inspiring experiences were taking students to places like Nigeria and India, working with local makers, and getting our hands dirty. Education should be about doing, experimenting, and mixing things up, not just sitting at a computer.

Y. I.: If we were to co-create a chair series, what kind of approach would excite you most?

M. G.: (Laughs) I feel a real connection with everything you've said. I'm not sure what the project is yet, but I think we should definitely collaborate on something, perhaps improvisational, narrative-driven, or tied to a specific place or community. The best collaborations come from shared curiosity and openness to new ideas.

Y. I.: Thank you so much, Martino. This has been incredibly inspirational. There's so much to expand on, and I feel like we should definitely work together.

M. G.: Thank you! And thanks for the link to Dilomprizulike [a.k.a. thejunkmanfromafrika]. He was amazing when we visited Lagos. Let's keep this conversation going.

CHAIRS
2006 — 2023

2006

W 40.00 cm
H 78.00 cm
D 94.00 cm

Two Become One is Yinka Ilori's first chair. It was made from two chairs and represents two lives merging. One chair came from a café, the other from a friend of Ilori. As their stories come together, they shape a new language and identity.

The chair was conceived during Ilori's studies at London Metropolitan University and marked the genesis of his creative practice. This was where storytelling began for him: a moment of exploring narrative freely and instinctively, guided only by how he felt about the chair itself. This curiosity opened his eyes to the hidden stories embedded in everyday objects. The green references hope and also nods to the green and white colour combination of the Nigerian flag.

COLLECTION: PARABLES

Parables features upcycled chairs and vividly showcases the storytelling power and captivating rhythms of Nigeria. Skillfully integrating the vibrant essence of Nigerian culture into his work, Ilori draws inspiration from "small parables with profound meanings" and the rich verbal traditions of his homeland.

L Oba (Yoruba for "King") merges Yinka Ilori's exploration of hierarchy and an inspiration from George Osodi's portraits of Nigerian monarchs. Wrapped in Aso Oke from Ondo State, Ilori's maternal heritage, the chair's cut and restored leg mirrors Osodi's vision of enduring cultural power: tradition rebalanced, dignity reclaimed.

2013

W 48.00 cm
H 78.00 cm
D 44.00 cm

R Iya (Yoruba for "Mother") honours maternal strength and tenderness. Missing slats, wrapped in African Wax print, evoke both imperfection and endurance, symbolising the unseen labour of mothers who remain steadfast and nurturing, even when carrying the weight of incompleteness.

2013

W –
H –
D –

L <u>Ijoko Agba</u> (Yoruba for "Big Man's Chair") embodies the Nigerian notion of the "Chairman", the respected boss or leader. Merging British design with African textiles, Yinka Ilori crafts a seat of dual heritage, where power, pride, and identity meet, celebrating the hybrid authority of one who sits between worlds.

2013

W –
H –
D –

R <u>Mobo</u> (Yoruba for "Freedom") embodies liberation and self-acceptance. Its open backrest and bird motifs evoke flight and release, while the cut and restored leg reflects the tension between personal freedom and the effort to find balance within society.

2013

W –
H –
D –

L Abike I (Yoruba for "Born to be pampered") represents care and affection. Their nonfunctional backrest resists utility, celebrating beauty without justification. Like a cherished person, they exist meaningfully in their own right, valued simply for being.

2013

W 40.00 cm
H 99.00 cm
D 62.00 cm

R Abike II (see Abike I)

2013

W 40.00 cm
H 100.00 cm
D 43.00 cm

L Abike III (see Abike I) 2013

W 95.00 cm
H 104.00 cm
D 42.00 cm

R Abike IV (see Abike I) 2013

W 40.00 cm
H 95.00 cm
D 43.50 cm

Let There Be Light reminds us not to judge others. Each rod, set at a different height, represents an individual on their own journey. The smallest rod holds a candle, its quiet light symbolising self-growth and the potential for transformation. Together, they affirm that every path has value and that focusing on your own journey allows others the space to shine in theirs.

2013

W 39.00 cm
H 60.00 cm
D 35.00 cm

Collection: Parables

L <u>Oba Kekere</u> (Yoruba for "Small King") features a standard design upholstered with traditional Nigerian Aso Oke fabric from Ondo State, Yinka's mother's homeland, lending the piece its cultural significance. One leg is cut off to reflect hierarchical status, with wooden pieces added back in to restore balance. Its intentionally shortened height, reminiscent of a child's chair, symbolises the societal position of youth or those considered "small" within a hierarchy.

<u>2013</u>

W 30.00 cm
H 58.00 cm
D 30.00 cm

R <u>Osumare</u> (Yoruba for "Rainbow") explores acceptance and the importance of embracing differences. Inspired by a friend opening up about his sexuality and masculinity, it reflects the emotional journey of finally expressing feelings that were long kept inside. The turned-down backrest symbolises the judgement people often face, being told their feelings are "wrong" when they are valid. The piece raises questions about sexuality and faith, challenging who has the authority to decide what is right or wrong.

<u>2014</u>

W 51.00 cm
H 52.00 cm
D 44.00 cm

COLLECTION: IT STARTED WITH A PARABLE

It Started with a Parable explores hierarchy and status through backrest heights, symbolising evolving personal strength, growth, and resilience. The chairs are adorned in African wax print (Ankara), tracing Indonesian batik origins and its African reinvention as a symbol of heritage and identity.

L	Threesacrowd merges the phrase "Three's a Crowd" and reflects on family relationships, particularly sibling dynamics. The seat is divided into three parts, representing the presence and connection of three individuals, yet it forms an union and an homage to the complexity of sibling relationships. Even with just three, it can feel like a full crowd: rich, loud, and familiar.		2013 W 46.00 cm H 45.00 cm D 50.00 cm
R	Ewa 'Àtùpà kì í níyì lọ̀ọ̀sán' ("Ewa" means "Beauty" in Yoruba and "Àtùpà kì í níyì lọ̀ọ̀sán" translates to "A lamp is not valued in the daytime".) This chair explores different definitions and perceptions of beauty. A lampshade adorns one chair, making it stand out and appear more beautified than the others. The design challenges traditional notions of what defines beauty and taste, with one chair leg intentionally cut off to reflect the hierarchy of beauty, and wooden pieces added back in as an attempt to restore balance.		2013 W – H – D –

Stacks becomes a metaphor for layered identity, each piece partially functional alone, yet together forming a complete, multifaceted expression of cultural intersection and belonging.

2013

W –
H –
D –

Odd One Out explores themes of hierarchy and status. The cut leg reflects social standing and imbalance within systems of power, while the added wooden element gestures toward an attempt to restore balance. The lowered backrest further signifies diminished hierarchy, inviting reflection on instability, inequity, and the structures that shape position within society.

2013

W –
H –
D –

Kekere (Yoruba for "Small") evokes childhood scale and children's place in society through shortened legs.

2013

W	–
H	–
D	–

Img. 14: “This Is Where It Started“ Exhibition, A Whitespace Creative Agency, Lagos, 2014. Courtesy A Whitespace Creative Agency.

COLLECTION: THIS IS WHERE IT STARTED

This Is Where It Started was exhibited at A Whitespace Creative Agency in Lagos in 2014, marking Yinka's first exhibition in West Africa and a homecoming presentation of his design practices, sponsored by Arts Council England and the British Council. The collection explores the journey of growth. It features chairs with varying backrest heights, reflecting differences in personal strength both within individuals and between people, acknowledging that some may not yet be at full strength. Through this, Ilori highlights strength as an evolving, developing quality over time.

Irungbon (Yoruba for "Beard") evokes swagger and status, reflected here in the moustache silhouette on the backrest.

2013

W 39.00 cm
H 60.00 cm
D 35.00 cm

Ife I (Yoruba for "Love") speaks to the care we extend to ourselves and to others as we grow. It presents the same chair in two different variants, representing different expressions of love yet remaining united by a shared grounding force. A sense of compassion runs through both, supporting individuals at every stage of their evolving strength.

2014

W 39.00 cm
H 77.00 cm
D 36.00 cm

Ife II (see Ife I) 2014

W 44.00 cm
H 75.00 cm
D 45.50 cm

Collection: This Is Where It Started

L Ife III (see Ife I) 2013

W 38.00 cm
H 73.50 cm
D 40.00 cm

R Ife IV (see Ife I) 2013

W 38.00 cm
H 73.50 cm
D 40.00 cm

Eyin —

2013

W 54.00 cm
H 93.00 cm
D 48.00 cm

Collection: This Is Where It Started

Baba Ibeta I–III are adorned in African wax print (Ankara), featuring a white cut-out representing the yam's sweet interior. Drawing from the parable, "No matter how hot your anger is, it cannot cook yams," the work explores patience and transformation, with plants symbolising growth.

2013

W 45.00 cm
H 89.00 cm
D 43.00 cm

Img. 15: Selection of chairs from Yinka Ilori's solo exhibition "Because the Truth Is Bitter", Just Africa Shop, Stockholm, 2014. Courtesy Yinka Ilori.

COLLECTION: BECAUSE THE TRUTH IS BITTER

Because the Truth Is Bitter reflects the proverb-like idea that harming a creature already seeking escape is both cruel and unnecessary. One paired set draws on a saying from Yinka's father about shielding children from harsh realities; shaped like a pair of ears, these chairs emphasise attentive listening and the weight of confronting difficult truths. Their sharp backrest conveys the bitterness or discomfort of reality, underscoring the tension between innocence and honesty. The other pair, inspired by a friend's coming-out journey, features a lampshade form that rises like a bridge, symbolising freedom, individuality, and the path toward self-acceptance. As a twin set, they embody close bonds and shared journeys, while acknowledging differences shaped by personal experience.

Stones Should Not Be Thrown at a Bird That Wants to Fly Away I — 2014

W 38.00 cm
H 73.50 cm
D 40.00 cm

Collection: Because the Truth Is Bitter

Stones Should Not Be Thrown at a Bird That Wants to Fly Away II — 2014

W 38.00cm
H 73.50cm
D 40.00cm

Eti I —

2014

W 46.00 cm
H 80.00 cm
D 40.00 cm

Collection: Because the Truth Is Bitter

Eti II — 2014

W 54.00 cm
H 74.00 cm
D 43.00 cm

COLLECTION: IF CHAIRS COULD TALK

If Chairs Could Talk honours the forgotten stories of discarded wooden chairs that Yinka Ilori found while exploring London. Spotting a chair destined for the skip from a bus ignited a passion to rescue these pieces, creating a growing collection at home. Ilori realised the significant influence chairs have on our perceptions of status, like thrones elevating one's position or cherished family chairs sparking childhood squabbles.

<u>Backbone</u> tells the story of a childhood friend who migrated from Nigeria to London. Intelligent yet disruptive, they navigated language barriers, cultural differences, and systemic challenges, becoming the "black sheep". The distorted form and black colour reflect these hardships, while the colourful seat celebrates their Nigerian heritage, a vibrant foundation that remained part of them throughout.

2015

W 39.00 cm
H 77.00 cm
D 36.00 cm

Collection: If Chairs Could Talk

Helping Hand tells the story of a friend with immense potential who needed support to flourish. Vibrant colours reveal the brightness that was always there beneath the surface, and the handle on the back symbolises the "helping hand" they should have received but didn't. It highlights the importance of recognising and supporting hidden potential.

2015

W 44.00 cm
H 75.00 cm
D 45.50 cm

L Flowerbomb represents a young school friend whose intelligence was initially overlooked, this chair embodies quiet growth and eventual flourishing. Like a late-blooming flower, the friend defied expectations and made a lasting impact, a reminder that growth happens in its own time.

2015

W 44.00 cm
H 75.00 cm
D 45.50 cm

R A Trapped Star tells the story of two brothers. The older, failed by the system, ended up in jail, while the younger, full of talent in football and music, tried to follow in his footsteps. Despite potential, both were let down by systemic failures. The chairs reflect their bond, shared path, and the tragedy of potential lost.

2015

W 45.00 cm
H 89.00 cm
D 43.00 cm

Collection: If Chairs Could Talk

Captain Hook represents another highly intelligent friend often overlooked by societal systems. Left to "dry out" without guidance, they eventually blossomed outside conventional structures, demonstrating that brilliance sometimes only needs the right space to grow.

2015

W 54.00 cm
H 109.00 cm
D 49.00 cm

COLLECTION: HOME AFFAIRS

Home Affairs reflects Yinka's Nigerian family life through vibrant patterns and bespoke Khanga textiles. Incorporating Nigerian and Swahili parables, it explores the tension of discussing private matters in public spaces, highlighting the dichotomy of private versus public life.

L Untitled — 2015

W 38.50 cm
H 77.00 cm
D 42.00 cm

R Ijoko Alejo — 2015

W 38.50 cm
H 77.00 cm
D 42.00 cm

Birds of a Same Feather — 2015

W 45.00 cm
H 81.00 cm
D 44.00 cm

Img. 16: "Do Good Because of Tomorrow" Programme, part of Common Ground at Milton Keynes Art Centre, 2016. Photo: Andy Stagg.

COLLECTION: DO GOOD BECAUSE OF TOMORROW

Do Good Because of Tomorrow embodies the concept of doing good today to benefit tomorrow. Small church-like windows in the chairs evoke reflection, morality, and spiritual guidance. The design encourages kindness as a daily practice, inspired by faith and lived experience, reminding viewers of compassion and community care.

Untitled — 2016

W 45.00 cm
H 79.00 cm
D 55.00 cm

Collection: Do Good Because of Tomorrow

L	Untitled	–	2016
			W 45.00 cm H 79.00 cm D 55.00 cm
R	Untitled	–	2016
			W 62.00 cm H 55.00 cm D 79.00 cm

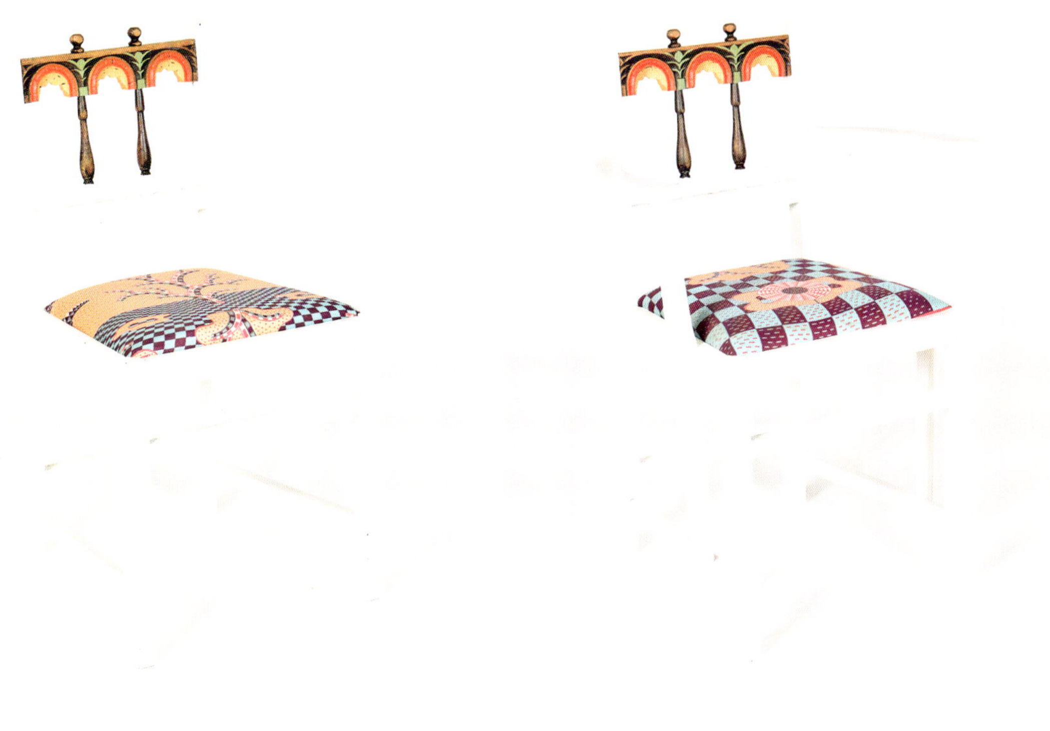

COLLECTION: A SWIMMING POOL OF DREAMS

A Swimming Pool of Dreams references Yinka's family trips to Margate alongside his fellow Pentecostal church members. These seaside trips were spiritual pilgrimages, filled with collective hopes and prayers. The collection embodies the dreams, longings, and whispered prayers of those who stood on Margate's shore, asking for change, healing, and miracles.

L **Iya Ati Moto** tells a story of a woman who longed for children, fulfilled through prayer, with a hinged wing symbolising both desire and realisation.

2016

W 50.20 cm
H 79.40 cm
D 44.90 cm

R **Untitled** –

2016

W 38.00 cm
H 76.00 cm
D 43.00 cm

Collection: A Swimming Pool of Dreams

L	Untitled	–	2016
			W 38.50 cm H 77.00 cm D 42.00 cm
R	Untitled	–	2016
			W 38.50 cm H 77.00 cm D 42.00 cm

What God Has Joined Together, Let No Man Put Asunder draws from biblical teachings; this chair celebrates family, shared values, and the strength of community. Integrated lyrics and gospel references connect spiritual, emotional, and cultural influences, while intersecting elements symbolise harmony and interconnectedness.

2017

W 38.50 cm
H 90.00 cm
D 80.00 cm

COLLECTION: TYPES OF HAPPINESS

Types of Happiness represents one of sixteen types of happiness. Hand-painted vibrant colours and patterns express a rollercoaster of emotions, giving each chair its own identity. Beneath the chair, the specific type of happiness is revealed, adding curiosity and play.

L Calmness – 2018

W 40.00 cm
H 100.00 cm
D 43.00 cm

R Determination – 2018

W 40.00 cm
H 100.00 cm
D 43.00 cm

W 40.00 cm
H 100.00 cm
D 43.00 cm

Happiness — 2018

W 40.00 cm
H 100.00 cm
D 43.00 cm

Collection: Types of Happiness

L Pride – 2018

W 40.00 cm
H 100.00 cm
D 43.00 cm

R Relaxation – 2018

W 40.00 cm
H 100.00 cm
D 43.00 cm

COLLECTION: INDIVIDUAL CHAIR EXPERIMENTS

Individual Chair Experiments explore identity through heavy themes of hierarchy and status, subjects that mattered to Ilori and that he found deeply compelling, particularly in early years. As his practice developed, his focus shifted. Through these objects, he began exploring how joy and community can be translated into form: through function, shape, material, and colour. Joy became a state of mind and a source of content. This marked a new chapter in which he created objects that embody beauty, optimism, and delight.

Eye Elóge (Yoruba for "Bird of Praise") was inspired by the power and beauty of the peacock—an animal whose full brilliance isn't always visible at first glance. Much like a performance, its beauty unfolds over time. This chair celebrates that concept: it's not just about function or structure, but about the moment when elegance emerges. The backrest becomes the stage for this transformation, revealing its ornamental form only after the core skeleton is in place.

2019

W 104.00 cm
H 77.00 cm
D 95.00 cm

Collection: Individual Chair Experiments

L In Your Own Time 'Ni Akoko Fe' radiates boldness and unapologetic energy, in contrast to earlier hidden narrative designs. Each chair embodies affirmation, resilience, and self-discovery while honouring Yinka's parents' migration from Nigeria to London and their unwavering optimism.

2020

W 40.00 cm
H 99.00 cm
D 43.00 cm

R Heavy Love 'Ife Eru' –

2020

W 40.00 cm
H 93.00 cm
D 43.00 cm

L	Point of Reflection	–	2020
			W 40.00 cm H 83.00 cm D 43.00 cm
R	Untitled V	–	2020
			W 40.00 cm H 99.00 cm D 62.00 cm

Collection: Individual Chair Experiments

Igbale —

2020

W 40.00 cm
H 95.00 cm
D 43.50 cm

COLLECTION: THERE IS GOOD IN ALL OF US

There Is Good in All of Us is a collection of chairs created in collaboration with luxury fashion brand MCM. Using upcycled chairs adorned with vibrant patterns and colours, Ilori conveys the idea that beauty and goodness lie beneath the surface. Central to the project is an invitation to look beyond appearances and recognise our shared humanity—symbolised by a kaleidoscope revealing the hidden beauty within us all.

Transparency 'Akoyawo' I references Yinka Ilori's parents, exploring their migration journey and the struggles and beauty within. Rough central cuts overlaid with resin reveal hidden pain and resilience, honouring the complexities of their experiences and legacy. Upholstered with MCM textiles in brown, black, pink, and blue-grey, it symbolises the experiences of migration faced by his parents.

2023

W 45.00 cm
H 80.00 cm
D 55.00 cm

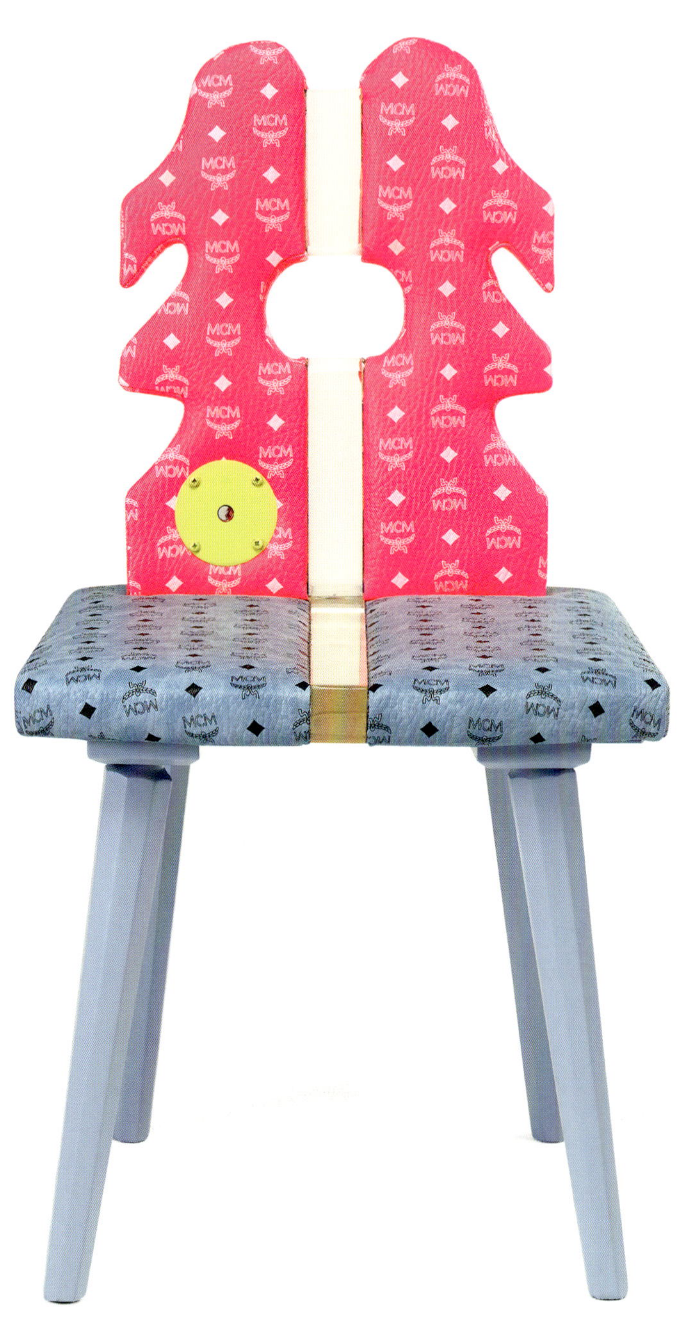

Collection: There Is Good in All of Us

Transparency 'Akoyawo' II (see Transparency 'Akoyawo' I) 2023

W 45.00 cm
H 80.00 cm
D 55.00 cm

Paint Me a Picture 'Ya Mi Awonan Kan' reconstructs visual memories of Nigeria from Yinka's childhood, featuring vibrant frames that pay tribute to his upbringing and ancestral home stories.

2023

W 47.00 cm
H 94.00 cm
D 41.00 cm

Collection: There Is Good in All of Us

We Are Magic 'Idan Ni Wa' features telescopes, celebrating the resilience, magic, and triumphs inherent in Black culture, embodying strength and enchantment.

2023

W 54.00 cm
H 74.00 cm
D 48.00 cm

<u>Big Shoes to Fill 'Bata Nla Lati Kun' I</u> is draped in gold MCM fabric, representing Yinka's older brother and highlighting the role model he is expected to be and the responsibility he carries within the family.

<u>2023</u>

W 35.00 cm
H 90.00 cm
D 55.00 cm

Collection: There Is Good in All of Us

Big Shoes to Fill 'Bata Nla Lati Kun' II is draped in cognac MCM fabric, symbolising the weight of family expectations, particularly on males. Each leg represents family members in an enduring legacy of responsibility.

2023

W 35.00 cm
H 90.00 cm
D 55.00 cm

Bright Shining Star 'Iraw Didan' is inspired by the idea of being a "bright shining star"—this chair reflects faith and determination, with lights representing parental belief in their children's potential.

2023

W 45.00 cm
H 79.00 cm
D 55.00 cm

Collection: There Is Good in All of Us

Point of Reflection 'Ojuami Ti Otito' symbolises Yinka Ilori's self-discovery, reflection, and pride in cultural heritage, inviting viewers to reflect on their own stories through mirrored forms and unique structure.

2023

W –
H –
D –

My Son Doesn't Belong Here 'Omo Mi Ko Wa Nibi' recalls a moment when Yinka's father advocated for his potential through its displaced backrest, a poignant reminder of parental love and belief in shaping a child's future.

2023

W –
H –
D –

Collection: There Is Good in All of Us

You Are Beautiful 'Olewa' is adorned with elegant lips, reminiscent of Dali's lips of Mae West,representing the enduring impact of Ilori's mother's affirmations. They remind us of the beauty, talent, and confidence that can flourish when a child is nurtured with love and encouragement.

2023

W –
H –
D –

COLLECTION: IYA NI WURA

Iya Ni Wura (Yorouba for “Mother is Gold”) celebrates the strength, beauty, and sacrifice of motherhood. The Rocking Chair fosters intimate mother–child moments, and the Bench brings family together, emphasising women’s importance as societal pillars. With handmade fabric by Hand & Lock reflecting Yinka’s upbringing, the three-piece collection was made to support Mothers2Mothers.

Rocking Chair — 2023

W 47.00 cm
H 88.00 cm
D 101.00 cm

Collection: Iya Ni Wura

2023

W 109.00 cm
H 89.60 cm
D 48.50 cm

Chair —

2023

W 62.00 cm
H 107.00 cm
D 68.00 cm

Collection: Iya Ni Wura

P	TITLE	Y	COLLECTION	DIMENSIONS
19	Two Become One	2006	–	W 40.00 · H 78.00 · D 94.00 cm
22	Oba	2013	Parables	W 48.00 · H 78.00 · D 44.00 cm
22	Iya	2013	Parables	–
23	Ijoko Agba	2013	Parables	–
23	Mobo	2013	Parables	–
24	Abike I	2013	Parables	W 40.00 · H 99.00 · D 62.00 cm
24	Abike II	2013	Parables	W 40.00 · H 100.00 · D 43.00 cm
25	Abike III	2013	Parables	W 95.00 · H 104.00 · D 42.00 cm
25	Abike IV	2013	Parables	W 40.00 · H 95.00 · D 43.50 cm
26	Let There Be Light	2013	Parables	W 39.00 · H 60.00 · D 35.00 cm
27	Oba Kekere	2013	Parables	W 30.00 · H 58.00 · D 30.00 cm
27	Osumare	2013	Parables	W 51.00 · H 52.00 · D 44.00 cm
30	Threesacrowd	2013	It Started with a Parable	W 46.00 · H 45.00 · D 50.00 cm
30	Ewa 'Àtùpà Kì Í Níyì Lóòsán'	2013	It Started with a Parable	–
31	Stacks	2013	It Started with a Parable	–
32	Odd One Out	2013	It Started with a Parable	–
33	Kekere	2014	It Started with a Parable	–
36	Irungbon	2014	This Is Where It Started	W 39.00 · H 60.00 · D 35.00 cm
37	Ife I	2014	This Is Where It Started	W 39.00 · H 77.00 · D 36.00 cm
38	Ife II	2014	This Is Where It Started	W 44.00 · H 75.00 · D 45.50 cm
39	Ife III	2014	This Is Where It Started	W 38.00 · H 73.50 · D 40.00 cm
39	Ife IV	2014	This Is Where It Started	W 38.00 · H 73.50 · D 40.00 cm
40	Eyin	2014	This Is Where It Started	W 54.00 · H 93.00 · D 48.00 cm
41	Baba Ibeta I	2014	This Is Where It Started	W 45.00 · H 89.00 · D 43.00 cm
41	Baba Ibeta II	2014	This Is Where It Started	W 45.00 · H 89.00 · D 43.00 cm
41	Baba Ibeta III	2014	This Is Where It Started	W 45.00 · H 89.00 · D 43.00 cm
44	Stones Should Not Be Thrown at a Bird That Wants to Fly Away I	2014	Because the Truth Is Bitter	W 38.00 · H 73.50 · D 40.00 cm
45	Stones Should Not Be Thrown at a Bird That Wants to Fly Away II	2014	Because the Truth Is Bitter	W 38.00 · H 73.50 · D 40.00 cm
46	Eti I	2014	Because The Truth Is Bitter	W 46.00 · H 80.00 · D 40.00 cm
47	Eti II	2014	Because The Truth Is Bitter	W 54.00 · H 74.00 · D 43.00 cm
50	Backbone	2015	If Chairs Could Talk	W 39.00 · H 77.00 · D 36.00 cm
51	Helping Hand	2015	If Chairs Could Talk	W 44.00 · H 75.00 · D 45.50 cm
52	Flowerbomb	2015	If Chairs Could Talk	W 44.00 · H 75.00 · D 45.50 cm
52	A Trapped Star	2015	If Chairs Could Talk	W 45.00 · H 89.00 · D 43.00 cm
53	Captain Hook	2015	If Chairs Could Talk	W 40.00 · H 109.00 · D 49.00 cm
56	Untitled	2015	Home Affairs	W 38.50 · H 77.00 · D 42.00 cm

P	TITLE	Y	COLLECTION	DIMENSIONS
56	Ijoko Alejo	2015	Home Affairs	W 38.50 · H 77.00 · D 42.00 cm
57	Birds of a Same Feather	2015	Home Affairs	W 45.00 · H 81.00 · D 44.00 cm
60	Untitled	2016	Do Good Because of Tomorrow	W 45.00 · H 79.00 · D 55.00 cm
61	Untitled	2016	Do Good Because of Tomorrow	W 45.00 · H 79.00 · D 55.00 cm
61	Untitled	2016	Do Good Because of Tomorrow	W 62.00 · H 55.00 · D 79.00 cm
64	Iya Ati Moto	2016	A Swimming Pool of Dreams	W 50.20 · H 79.40 · D 44.90 cm
64	Untitled	2016	A Swimming Pool of Dreams	W 38.00 · H 76.00 · D 43.00 cm
65	Untitled	2016	A Swimming Pool of Dreams	W 38.50 · H 77.00 · D 42.00 cm
65	Untitled	2016	A Swimming Pool of Dreams	W 38.50 · H 77.00 · D 42.00 cm
67	What God Has Joined Together, Let No Man Put Asunder	2017	–	W 38.50 · H 90.00 · D 80.00 cm
70	Calmness	2018	Types of Happiness	W 40.00 · H 100.00 · D 43.00 cm
70	Determination	2018	Types of Happiness	W 40.00 · H 100.00 · D 43.00 cm
71	Strength	2018	Types of Happiness	W 40.00 · H 100.00 · D 43.00 cm
72	Happiness	2018	Types of Happiness	W 40.00 · H 100.00 · D 43.00 cm
73	Pride	2018	Types of Happiness	W 54.00 · H 74.00 · D 43.00 cm
73	Relaxation	2018	Types of Happiness	W 40.00 · H 100.00 · D 43.00 cm
76	Eye Elóge	2019	Individual Chair Experiments	W 104.00 · H 77.00 · D 95.00 cm
77	In Your Own Time 'Ni Akoko Fe'	2020	Individual Chair Experiments	W 40.00 · H 99.00 · D 43.00 cm
77	Heavy Love 'Ife Eru'	2020	Individual Chair Experiments	W 40.00 · H 93.00 · D 43.00 cm
78	Point of Reflection	2020	Individual Chair Experiments	W 40.00 · H 83.00 · D 43.00 cm
78	Untitled V	2020	Individual Chair Experiments	W 40.00 · H 99.00 · D 62.00 cm
79	Igbale	2020	Individual Chair Experiments	W 40.00 · H 95.00 · D 43.50 cm
82	Transparency 'Akoyawo' I	2023	There Is Good in All of Us	W 45.00 · H 80.00 · D 55.00 cm
83	Transparency 'Akoyawo' II	2023	There Is Good in All of Us	W 45.00 · H 80.00 · D 55.00 cm
84	Paint Me A Picture 'Ya Mi Awonan Kan'	2023	There Is Good in All of Us	W 47.00 · H 94.00 · D 41.00 cm
85	We Are Magic 'Idan Ni Wa'	2023	There Is Good in All of Us	W 54.00 · H 74.00 · D 48.00 cm
86	Big Shoes to Fill 'Bata Nla Lati Kun' I	2023	There Is Good in All of Us	W 35.00 · H 90.00 · D 55.00 cm
87	Big Shoes to Fill 'Bata Nla Lati Kun' II	2023	There Is Good in All of Us	W 35.00 · H 90.00 · D 55.00 cm
88	Bright Shining Star 'Iraw Didan'	2023	There Is Good in All of Us	W 45.00 · H 79.00 · D 55.00 cm
89	Point of Reflection 'Ojuami Ti Otito'	2023	There Is Good in All of Us	–
90	My Son Doesn't Belong Here 'Omo Mi Ko Wa Nibi'	2023	There Is Good in All of Us	–
91	You Are Beautiful 'Olewa'	2023	There Is Good In All of Us	–
94	Rocking Chair	2023	Iya Ni Wura	W 48.00 · H 77.00 · D 101.00 cm
95	Bench	2023	Iya Ni Wura	W 109.00 · H 89.60 · D 48.50 cm
96	Chair	2023	Iya Ni Wura	W 62.00 · H 107.00 · D 68.00 cm

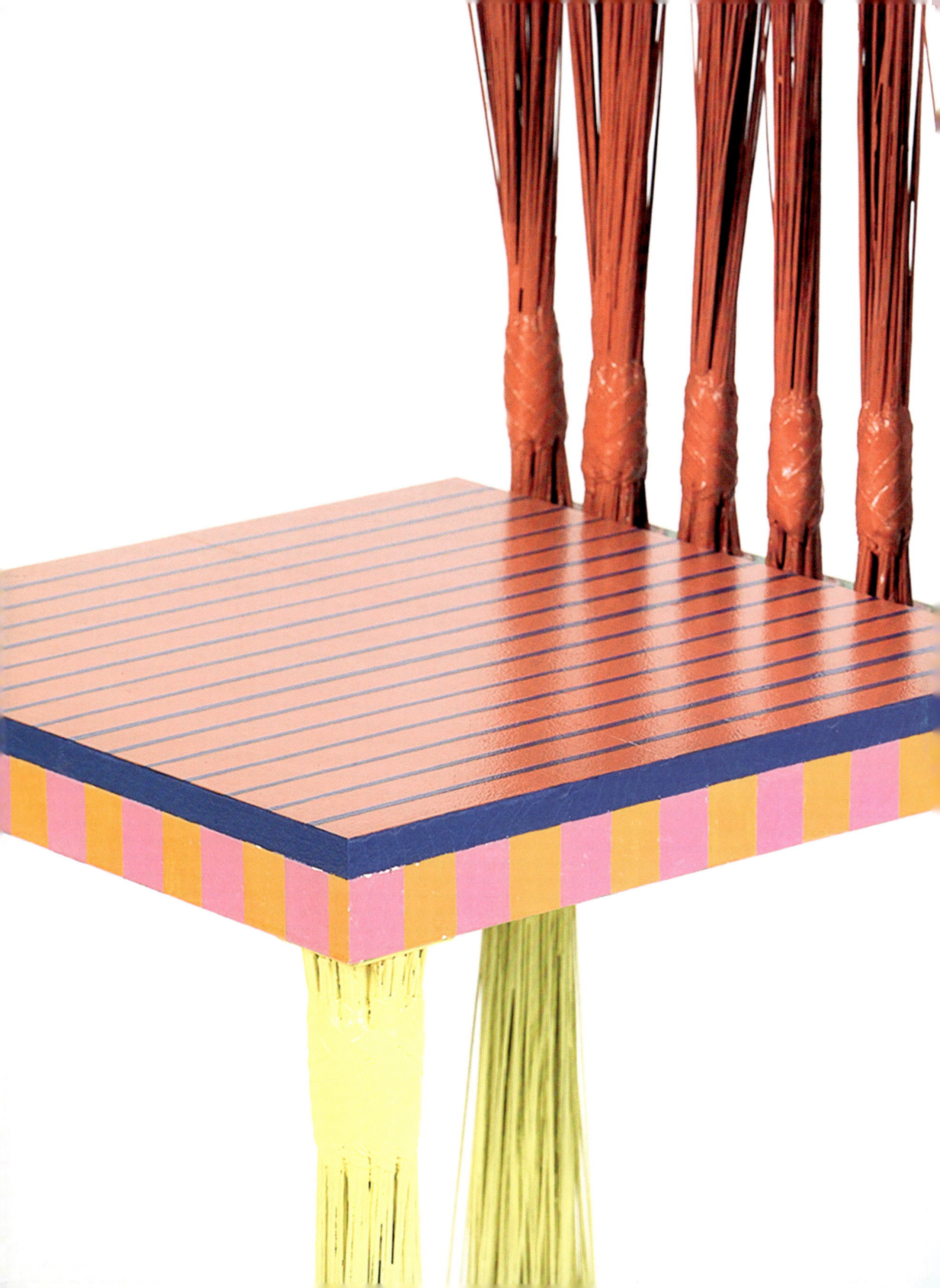

MCM

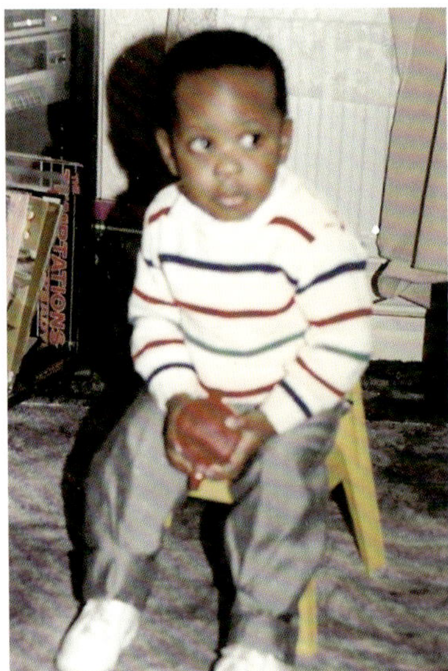

Img. 17: Yinka Ilori as a child, in his childhood home in North London. Courtesy Yinka Ilori.

Img. 18: Yinka Ilori's grandmother, photographed in Ondo State, Nigeria. Courtesy Yinka Ilori.

Img. 19: Yinka Ilori's beloved mother, Jhalobia Recreation Park and Gardens, Lagos, Nigeria, January 2024. Courtesy Yinka Ilori.

JULIANKNXX

CHAIRMAN

(No Dey Carry Last)

Before thrones learned to carry men,
before wood bent into obedience,
before crowns and titles,
the ground was the first throne.
Stones already knew whose weight
belonged to them.
Some men chase height,
calling themselves important.
But when *Chairman* enters,
his presence sits before his body.
The room rearranges itself.
Stools shift. Benches shuffle.
Even fallen trees adjust.
People go whisper:
Who be dat?
And another go answer:
Na Chairman–
wey no dey carry last.
Even if he sits on stone,
na that stone
go feel proud.

Yinka Ilori is a British-Nigerian multi disciplinary artist and designer whose vibrant work fuses his Nigerian heritage with a joyful, community-driven design ethos. He studied Furniture and Product Design at London Metropolitan University (2006–2009) and began his practice around 2011, initially upcycling vintage furniture in London.

Growing up in Islington, North London, to Nigerian immigrant parents, Ilori was profoundly influenced by bright African textiles, the Owambe party aesthetic, Sunday dress, and the storytelling culture of his heritage. These early experiences shaped his belief that design should be accessible, inclusive, and joyful. His practice employs bold colour palettes and patterns to celebrate identity, memory, and community.

Through studio work and public commissions, Ilori transforms furniture, architectural spaces, and urban environments into interactive, vibrant experiences. Notable projects include large-scale chairs from "Types of Happiness" for London's The Line art walk and a solo exhibition at the Design Museum. His work often draws on Nigerian parables and oral traditions, presenting design as a storytelling medium that engages diverse audiences. Recognised for his contribution to design, Ilori was awarded an MBE (Member of the Order of the British Empire) for services to design and diversity.

Based in West London, Ilori continues to produce work that brightens everyday environments, fosters connections, and elevates underrepresented perspectives in design.

CHAIRS IN PUBLIC COLLECTIONS

Img. 13: Yinka Ilori in his studio, North Acton, London, 2025. Photo: Lewis Khan.

My love of chairs started from an early age. Anything I was sitting on, a car seat, a chair, a tricycle seat, I was obsessed with. There was something about being held by a seat that captured me.

I've always loved the family and communal act of sitting together, the way a chair can hold a conversation without saying a single word. That feeling has followed me from childhood into adulthood.

I've found beauty and hidden stories inside objects. Chairs became the objects I trusted with my stories; stories about family, and about the people I love. Over the years, they have become sources of joy, comfort, and meaning for me.

Chairs have shown up in so many celebratory moments: the sea of chairs in church, symbolic and spiritual, where people prayed, knelt, touched, and hoped; and at home, in my parents' house parties in our small London flat, where monoblock chairs became beacons of joy, holding people as they ate, laughed, cried, cuddled, and sang.

And then there are the quieter memories. My parents sitting on chairs in the immigration office, waiting to learn their fate as they hoped to be granted an indefinite stay in the United Kingdom. That image has stayed with me to this day.

For me, chairs are symbols of hope, joy, confusion, and anxiety, each one tied to a specific memory. They are an integral part of my life, my family's life, and the lives of the people I love.

In this book, it was important for me to explore the power of chairs, whether through hierarchy, status, or deeply personal moments. Chairs may be seen as objects of power, but they also hold our emotions. We cry on chairs. We argue on chairs. We love on chairs. Chairs are witnesses to our lives. We shouldn't take them for granted.

I hope that as you read this book and dive into its stories, you discover something magical that resonates with you; something you can carry with you and share with others.